LOOK AND FIND®

ELMO

This book is brought to you by
the letter M and the number 10!

Illustrated by Art Mawhinney

Cover illustration by DiCicco Studios

Written by Catherine McCafferty and Brooke Zimmerman

Visit us on the Web at **www.sesamestreet.com**

Published by
Louis Weber, C.E.O.
Publications International, Ltd.
7373 North Cicero Avenue
Lincolnwood, Illinois 60712

www.pubint.com

Manufactured in China.

8 7 6 5 4 3 2 1

ISBN 0-7853-5990-7

publications international, ltd.

One bright, sunny morning on Sesame Street, Elmo heard a toe-tapping kind of music he'd never heard before. As Elmo hummed along, he began to feel very curious. Where was the happy-sounding music coming from? Maybe it was from a toy in his toy box!

Can you help Elmo find the letter M, the number 10, and toys that make music?

10

The number 10

M

M is for MUSIC!

toy piano

trumpet

cymbals

tambourine

ukulele

drum

Bomm–ba–da–domm. Elmo listened closely. The music was coming from outside! Elmo ran down to the courtyard, following the sound. There, children and monsters were playing and singing. They were making music, but it wasn't the same.

While Elmo was outside, he noticed a lot of things with strings. Can you spot them too?

There are 10 yo-yos. Can you find all 10?

M is for marionette

clothesline

kite

paddleball

ball of yarn

Elmo thought he heard some more music coming from Hooper's Store, so he went inside to check it out. Zoe showed Elmo a music box that was playing the pretty tune. But it was not the same sound Elmo had heard earlier that morning.

Hooper's Store was very crowded because there was a big sale. Look around the crowd to find:

Bert and the number 10

M is for music box

The Count

Baby Bear

Betty Lou

Cookie Monster

Rosita

Grover

As Elmo walked down Sesame Street to continue his search for the super-groovy music, he heard some terrible crashing and banging sounds. It was Oscar the Grouch and his all-Grouch band! (Nothing is noisier!) CLANG! BANG! SLAM!

Oscar's music was so loud, it shook the trash right out of his can! It may look like junk, but to Oscar, it's treasure. Can you find this terrific trash?

There are 10 tin cans. Can you find all 10?

MILK

M is for milk

racket

tire

shoe

lamp

pillow

Elmo followed the music to 123 Sesame Street. Elmo definitely heard music there. No wonder, because Ernie was singing to Rubber Duckie. It's fun to make music and bubbles at bathtime!

Elmo and Ernie make a splash playing with bath toys. Lots of duckie friends have come to visit! Can you find these?

There are 10 baby duckies. Can you find all 10?

M is for mop

Trucker Duckie

Lucky Duckie

Grubby Duckie

Duckleberry Swim

Bubble Duckie

Construction Duckie

Elmo began to wonder if he would ever find the music he'd heard before. So he asked Big Bird for help. Big Bird was listening to his favorite kind of music: bird songs! The air was filled with chirps and tweets, whistles and trills.

As the twittery tune played, birds came to listen. Can you find these feathered friends?

10 baby birds in 1 nest

M is for mockingbird

Little Bird

early bird

lovebirds

catbird

blue bird

birdbrain

Maybe someone at the park would know where the mystery music was coming from. Elmo headed that way, but a traffic jam of ice cream trucks stopped him in his tracks. Each truck played a tune, but none was the music Elmo wanted to hear.

Look around for these yummy frozen treats:

There are 10 ice pops. Can you find all 10?

M is for mint ice cream

ice cream sandwich

twist cone

snow cone

strawberry sundae

banana split

Elmo stopped to think. It seemed he had looked everywhere, and still couldn't find that morning's marvelous melody. But wait! There was music coming from the park!

At long last, Elmo had found the toe-tapping tune he had been looking and listening for all day. What a great sound! Look around and find all 10 "M" bands!

moo band

monster band

mouse band

mandolin band

moose band

monkey band

mermaid band

marching band

magician band

mariachi band

Looking in his toybox made Elmo want to play. Should he play music? Or a sport? Go back to Elmo's room and find these fun, sporty toys. Let's play!

baseball

football

baseball bat

soccer ball

Let's have fun playing and singing outside. Can you find the things the children and monsters are singing about?

I'm a Little **Teapot**

Mary Had a Little **Lamb**

There's a Hole in My **Bucket**

Duckies are just one kind of bird that likes water. Go back to Ernie's bathroom and find these other water-loving birds:

swan

flamingo

pelican

Birds aren't the only things that fly. If you buzz back to Big Bird's nest, you're bound to find these bugs:

bees

butterfly

beetle

Bert is buying paperclips for 10¢ at Hooper's Store. Can you find these other super-sale prices?

5¢ 50¢

75¢ 25¢

Oscar thinks all his trash is treasure. Can you look through the junk to find some pieces of **real** treasure?

ring

coin

crown

Fruity flavors are delicious. Go back to the playground and find:

grapes

pineapple

banana

apple

When it comes to music, listening is lovely. But dancing is divine! Can you find these three happy dancers in the park?